LIVE IN PEACE

LIVE IN PEACE

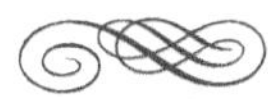

*Intentionally live
your best life.*

CHA-MARIE AVERETT MORGAN

Cha-Marie Averett Morgan

Foreword

"Twenty-five years, fifty countries, and countless contacts, what a blessing it is to have encountered so many people through this networking journey. But, as I think about "faces and places" over my career, Chami is one of those dynamic personalities that stands out. She is a rare combination of determination and inspiration packed into a truly genuine soul. Her love of people and life has been at the heart of her drive. Cha-Marie has a true grit for learning, growing, and helping others do the same. Her first book is reflective of its author. An intimate look into what has shaped her passions, pursuits, and the valuable perspective she has gained. "Live in Peace" gives an insightful narrative to a mission we all aspire to. I thoroughly enjoy and recommend this book. It offers both captivating moments of entertainment paired with earnest enlightenment. Read it. Enjoy it. Live it."

Kevin Moore

Global Entrepreneur and Found Distributor

"I have had the opportunity to speak in 20 different countries, write 8 books and host 25 different mastermind events. Through-out these events, Chami has attended as many events as any one of the students with the exception of 2 people. I have seen her growth but what she doesn't know is that through our masterminds I have learned a tremendous amount from her. She is constantly challenging new ideas and concepts. She is constantly quick to take action. She is raw, honest, and vulnerable. Throughout this book, Chami does an excellent job at teaching you how to find peace.

Each chapter could an entire book on its own. This is a book you will want to read over and over again. This is a book that will help you in all aspects of your life including both your relationships and your business. Don't just read it! Study it!"

Rob Sperry
8x Author and Public Speaker

Content

Introduction

Live In Peace

A little over a year ago a well-known celebrity passed away. All throughout social media, I saw Rest In Peace (R.I.P). As I pondered his life and his possible moments before death, I couldn't help but think... 'I don't want to just die in peace, I want to *live* in peace!' From that thought have come hundreds of additional thoughts that have led me here, to write this book. I am excited for you to join me on this journey as I share tools that can lead you into a life filled with peace!

"Our prime purpose in life is to help others, and if you can't help them, at least don't hurt them."

~Dalai Lama

I

Safe Spaces

In an ideal world, your family, extended family, and friends would all be a part of that circle of trust where you know you have a safe space. Where you can make mistakes, screw up, say the wrong thing, and still experience unconditional love and acceptance.

Sadly, for many of us, that circle of trust, that safe space, is small. But that's ok. Quality over quantity.

Also, *you* can be your own safe space!!!!!

We are all human and at one point or another, we will let each other down and disappoint. And often it will be with those we love the most and are closest to.

Be your own safe space thru self-awareness, honesty, and trust. Journal writing might be beneficial for you. You are in your own head. You know what you say about yourself, think about yourself, and how you treat yourself. If you have let yourself down, no matter the reason, it's not too late. Decide today to be the best version of yourself. And work on that every single day.

For those of you blessed to have a safe space, use it. Talk things out. Share your thoughts and insights. Your good, bad, and ugly truths.

As a parent, my hope is that my kids always view me as a safe space. I've learned I cannot control who else is in that safe space, but I can provide the love and trust necessary to show they are safe with me.

I think an important way to be a safe space for both yourself and others is to be willing to take ownership and admit when you've made a mistake. People may or may not accept your apology. That's up to them and out of your control. If you find you struggle to apologize, ask yourself why.

Those unwilling to apologize are often struggling with their own EGO. This is not something you can "fix" for anyone but yourself.

Before moving on to the next chapter, let me just share a word of caution. Not all those you would like to be, will be a safe space. If you know or question or wonder if the information you share will be shared with others or used against you somehow/someday/someway, then that is NOT a safe space. I am a trusting and loyal person and often expect the same in others. So, be cautious and intentional in choosing who you welcome into your circle of trust. There's a book I highly recommend when it comes to dealing with toxic people in your life by Dr. Sherrie Campbell called "But it's your Family".

Sadly, I've had to learn the hard way that those you love and wish you could trust, are not guaranteed safe spaces. You can still love and maintain healthy friendships while not letting them into your circle of trust.

"Gratitude turns what we have into enough."

~Anonymous

2

Gratitude

Growing up, I was always a positive/high-energy person! I'm naturally happy *most* of the time!!!! It wasn't till I became a married adult and started working in the network marketing industry that I learned that what came naturally to me, wasn't exactly something that came naturally to others!!! I was in my 3rd company and a LOT of things were going wrong!!! Many, many products were out of stock and there was a lot of complaining. It was difficult for several months for us as distributors. It was in those circumstances that I recognized that gift within myself to look for the good! I knew that while frustrating, it was going to be an amazing situation for the future of the company. Most of my customers had no idea the struggles the distributors were facing!

Positivity may come naturally to me, but what about those of you who struggle?

My answer is simple. Gratitude.

You've probably heard it time and time again and believe it's some "la la la" answer. But it genuinely works.

A year ago I was in a dark headspace. I was struggling emotionally, physically, and mentally and felt as though all the things I was going through were out of my control. And some were. I have been taught to embrace the suck but to not stay stuck in the suck. So, I allowed myself to feel. I allowed myself the safe space to process. I felt I had to be strong for my husband and kids, but I also knew I needed to face the struggles I was facing and not bury them.

I started writing 3 things I was grateful for, EVERY SINGLE DAY.

It wasn't right away, and I can't even tell you the "when", but eventually life got good again. I recognized what was within my control, and what was out of my control and took ownership of my actions and reactions.

It was so refreshing!!!!

If you want a positive life, look for ways to be grateful. You'll start noticing the small and wonderful things that are a part of your everyday life, but so often get overlooked. You may start with the simple but important things like:

- I'm grateful for the shower I was able to take today.

- I'm grateful for the food in our pantry.
- I'm grateful for how I handled a difficult moment with my kid!
- I'm grateful to breathe.

Those little things begin to paint the bigger picture of your life. Your happiness matters! There is so much to be grateful for!

I feel a component that can affect gratitude is expectation. We often have expectations and when they are not met, we are disappointed, discouraged, hurt, or frustrated.

With family members, set clear expectations. If you have a need that isn't being met, discuss it. I will tell you, there are some expectations we have that others are incapable of meeting. Some choose not to meet it, while others legitimately don't know how.

My husband is the youngest of six boys. I'd hoped to feel protected and defended by my husband, but I was expecting something he couldn't give. He didn't know how to defend himself, much less someone else.

We lived near family for the first year, then moved away for the next 6 years. When we moved back, there were expectations on both sides. My hubby suggested a family meeting to discuss what work-life looked like for him. He works for the government and has odd hours. We personally love how his schedule works, and we're used to it, but it takes some figuring out for others. He reached out and was told it wasn't necessary... Boy oh boy do we regret not pushing that more. For several years he worked Friday and Saturday nights and middays on Sundays. There was hurt and frustration that he couldn't attend many family functions. It was expected that he would re-arrange his schedule or call in sick, and that's not his work ethic. Sadly, much of that has remained unresolved and we continue to focus on our own little family.

Our hope was that living near family would mean coming to and attending our kids' sporting events. It turned out that how close we lived didn't change the support for this.

After several years of frustration and hurt, I decided to go to counseling. I was in a place where I thought our only options were to move or disown. In counseling, I was given tools on how to better manage my expectations. I learned to set boundaries. There were some expectations we weren't willing to meet, and that was our choice, just as them not being willing to meet some of our expectations. We all have choices.

I'm so grateful for the understanding I now have about boundaries and expectations. Putting and keeping these in place will absolutely allow for a more peace-filled life.

From all of the experiences we've had so far, we've learned to enjoy and be grateful for the relationships we do have. The time we are able to spend with those we love. Focusing on what is great, is so much better than focusing on what isn't the way you envisioned it to be. We have family that lives away and we often will only get to see them for one or two days of their vacation. We've learned to take what we can get and embrace it! We enjoy the time we do have rather than focusing on what we don't get.

"I embraced the unknown and lived there until it became known to me. And once the unknown became known, not only did it change my life- it became very precious to me."

~Rob Sperry

"Trust the wait.
Embrace the uncertainty.
Enjoy the beauty of becoming."

~Unknown

3

Embrace

Embrace was a word I chose to carry with me throughout 2020. Little did I know, or any of us know, what 2020 would bring to our lives.

The word embrace was definitely inspired. Instead of focusing on the fear and chaos that surrounded me, I chose to look for the good and embrace my life.

While 2020 was very difficult and draining, I was able to find so much good and there was so much to be grateful for. There were some difficult extended family experiences I had, and because of the pandemic, I was able to process, sort thru, and handle them, rather than brushing them under the rug and trying to forget. I was able to lean on my husband and more fully embrace his presence in my life. He was and continues to be my rock.

We are imperfect human beings with life experiences that we navigate and process and learn from as we go. Each experience shapes our perspective. I am a big reader and am a fan of Amish "love" stories. I love that it's exciting to see if they will hold hands. One of the biggest things I've pulled from these types of books is the Amish have a very real and beautiful understanding of accepting God's will. When in the midst of a trial or struggle, it often becomes difficult to see that this will somehow be for your benefit and good. But I ultimately believe this to be true. The struggles we face help us build character. Help shape us. Help us see our strength. We can trust that life will work out for the best.

A respected and talented mental performance coach, Nicole Detling, taught me, Embrace the Suck, but don't stay stuck in the suck. Too often we brush things under the rug, ignore them and hope they go away, but we must embrace all of our experiences. To learn from them. To grow thru what you go thru. Staying stuck there is a choice. We must intentionally hold space for ourselves as we process and then allow ourselves grace in moving forward.

When life goes away from our expectations, we often fight it, and I encourage you to choose to embrace it. Embrace the change. Embrace learning and growing. Embrace your life. Embrace who you are, your purpose, your divine nature, and your destiny! Each and every day is a fresh, new start! Let go of what went wrong yesterday, last week, and last year and embrace and live in the NOW!

"Abundance comes from within. It comes from thought, intention, attention, and expectation."

~Deepak Chopra

"You don't need a new day, a new life, a new spouse, a new home, a new car to be happy or to start over.

You need a new Mindset."

~Anonymous

4

Abundance Mindset

I am a strong believer in the power of the mind.

When I was a kid, I played soccer. My Dad would ask how many goals I was going to score and I would give him a number before each game, and sure enough, that's how many I'd score! My hubby grew up doing the same thing! And still to this day it works for him. I've found that we often lose that confidence as we grow up. But my hubby still has it, and it especially shows when we are playing a family game called Aggravation. If you haven't played, you are missing out!!! There are marbles and dice. The goal is to get your four marbles around the board into your home base!!! My husband is stealthy. He distracts and makes everyone else the target while he slowly starts winning the game. Ugh. Then, he'll be getting his very last guy into home and will need whatever number! Let's say a 3! He'll shake the dice in his hands and exclaim, "And THAT'S the GAME!" and he will *legit* roll a 3!!! I've seen this happen more times than I can count.

While life isn't as simple as rolling a dice to decide on your next move, your belief in yourself plays a big role in what you will be able to accomplish.

So many hold back because they don't believe they can accomplish their goal. So many let fears take over their decision-making.

If you know that you grew up with a toxic or unhealthy mindset, I urge you to notice what those are and work on them. Rewrite your script. Your brain is constantly trying to prove your beliefs as true. Find a coach or mentor! Sometimes talking this out is a great step toward personal healing and growth.

Instead of being afraid to fail, be afraid to not try. View failure as a learning opportunity rather than an end of the world scenario!

Abundance and Scarcity Mindsets are the two most known and widely talked about. Consider how each of these present themselves in your life?

Abundance vs. scarcity mindsets are actively apart of your life. If you already know that, this chapter will be so much easier to understand. Peace is so much clearer when you think abundantly. There's enough success, love, money, friendship and so on for everyone!!!!

The best way I can express this is by having more than one kid!!!

As a first-time parent, you love that kiddo so much and just can't comprehend having that much love for anything or anyone else! Then you have your second kiddo! The love expands!!!! It doesn't divide. You don't suddenly love your first child a little less so you can give some love to the second!

In life, there are far too many who want "fair" and this is a scarcity mindset. Just because someone experiences a win or success doesn't mean you somehow lose!!!!

I choose each and every day to cheer others on in their journey!!! We all need that and could use more of it!

Scarcity is the opposite of abundance. It's the belief that you are always getting shorthanded, nothing is fair, and everything others accomplish somehow diminishes your accomplishments. Scarcity will drag you into a dark space where gratitude becomes difficult to find and peace does not exist.

An example in my own life was when I was in college. A boyfriend had recently proposed to me, broke up with me, proposed again and broke up with me again...Rollercoaster for another time, and maybe another book. During one of these downs, I had a roomate get engaged! Ring, cute story, and all! I "should" have been happy for her. And normally, I believe I'm the kind of person that would have. However, in my scarcity mindset and the drama revolving around my relationship with this boy, I was bitter. It wasn't "fair". It sounds so ridiculous to me, even as I type. But that was how I handled it. I was immature. It was unnecessary, and at the time very real to me.

Because we are human, there will be times when you or someone you know is impossible to please. The "enough is never enough" frame of mind. This is often a red flag of narcissism along with a scarcity mindset. While I could probably write a chapter on that, it's not a subject that I have answers that will lead to peace. The narcissts in my life are not active members of my life. Keep in mind, that we as adults do not have the power to hold other adults accountable.

If you believe yourself to be in a scarcity mindset, look for abundance, blessings, and the gifts you have in your life. They are there. You will find what you focus on. So, if your focus is "life isn't fair", your brain is going to continue to find reasons this is true. Don't let it. Rewire your mind. Find the joy in others' successes.

"Deserve". A Roadblock I've found with abundance is the questioning if you deserve or are worthy. I'll be honest. I struggle with the word deserve. I personally view it as a similiar word to entitlement. I believe all people "deserve" peace, joy, and fulfillment. Beyond that, I feel people overuse and stretch what they believe they deserve.

Those who feel they "deserve" a better job, a promotion, or a pay raise, but do nothing on their end to improve, grow, or better themselves... that's not how abundance works! Sitting on our thumbs and wishing good things to come our way is not how the universe works.

I do believe you start achieving and growing more when you believe you are capable and worthy, and decide to put in the work.

You deserve all that you work to achieve. You deserve to have a healthy relationship with yourself. On a plane, you're told to do your face mask first. That's the same with life, mindset, and abundance. Until you believe in yourself, you won't be able to fully give of yourself to others.

"Comparison is the biggest thief of your journey and the greatest distractor of your time."

~Anonymous

5

Comparing

For so long I have thought that comparing is a "woman" thing, but I will tell you, it's a "human" thing. We MUST remember that we are all on our own journey. My win doesn't equal your loss. And your success doesn't take away my opportunity to have success!

It's so important we recognize that we each have a very personal purpose. We are here on this earth to learn and to grow. The life each of us leads is very specifically ours.

While we often can relate, none of us experience the *EXACT* same situation in the *exact* same way, with the *exact* same reactions and emotions.

That's not how life works.

But we can learn from one another. We can cheer each other on in this journey called life.

We sometimes want what others have... We've all experienced this probably a time or two... or three. And for the most part, it's human and normal. How far we go with it and how deep our envy goes is where it becomes dangerous to our own personal growth and success. I recently learned to take a different look at jealousy. Jealousy can help you know what it is you really want.

Instead of spending time wishing we had what others have, we need to put in the work to get to where we want to go.

I had a recent experience where I was comparing and didn't even know it. I was at a Mastermind and had received some incredible training, by a young, good-looking, knowledgeable man. After taking group and individual pictures, I had the nerve to tell the guy, well not in these specific words, but the jest of it was, "you must know a big part of why you're great at door to door sales is because you are so good looking"...

WHAT was I thinking? I could tell it caught him off guard, and it's not uncommon for me to have open mouth insert foot moments, but this one was not normal for me. Afterward, I couldn't believe how petty and rude I'd been.

As I tried to figure out what in the world would bring me to say this to this man who has had phenomenal success, and yes he's good-looking, but he's also very skilled. He is a leader that can teach and implement.

It took about an hour before it dawned on me. It was my personal issue. It had nothing to do with him. In my mind, I've always believed I'd have more success if I was beautiful. I think of myself as pretty, but not beautiful, not gorgeous, not stunning, and not breathtaking. For years, I've subconsciously told myself that beauty was what I was lacking in order to have the success I desired.

This is Scarcity. This is Comparison. Not abundance. Comparison will not bring you peace.

I did apologize to this man, and am not proud of what I said, but am very grateful for the insight it gave me.

Recognizing these insecurities within ourselves is so very important. We aren't ever going to be perfect, but we can strive to always do better. Be better. Better today than yesterday.

Put on those blinders, dig deep, and keep moving forward. Start with the end in mind. Where are you trying to go? What is it that you truly want? Work backward and make a game plan of how to get there.

"When you blame others, you give up your power to change."

~Anonymous

6

Victim

I'm betting you have someone in your life that, *no matter what* finds something to complain about, find fault in, or view as unfair. Another wonderful aspect of being human! While some feed off of this, for others, this is all they know. Until they see or are taught differently, they live in this victim state of mind. And I will tell you, there is no peace there.

Here are a few questions you can ask yourself to gauge if you are in a Victim mindset.

- Do you catch yourself complaining often?
- Do you hide your emotions?
- Do you believe others don't notice you or pay attention to you?

- Do you assume others are talking about you behind your back?
- Do you talk about yourself often?
- Do you bring situations up over and over again that you are seeking validation for?
- Do you often think about the ways people "owe" you?
- Do you use phrases like "after all that I've done for them" or "that's not fair".

If you answered yes to 3 or more of these, then it's likely you are currently in a victim mindset.

DON'T worry!!! All of us have spent time there at some point or another. The key is to choose to not *stay* there. Recognize, resolve, and move forward the best you can.

I highly recommend Rob Sperry's book, "The Game of Conquering". It's a great blueprint on how to process and work thru the different mindsets! While I don't have a desire to rewrite what has already been a powerful book in my life, I will share some examples where I've been in Victim, Survivor, and Conqueror Mindsets.

Victim

In a later chapter, I will share more about a relationship that wasn't serving me. For here, I will explain that while the relationship was toxic and unhealthy, for many years I was choosing to remain the victim. I made excuses for why I was remaining attached to a relationship that was hurtful and disrespectful. It is easy to play the victim and sometimes feels good to think "I'll keep trying" and "I'm doing my part" and "at least I can say I've made efforts". HOWEVER, by staying in the victim role, I wasn't growing. I was stuck.

I was recently told, "you aren't 'stuck', you are just afraid to make the necessary changes." How true that was. I was afraid of the judgment, opinions of others, and backlash I would receive for "giving up" and "cutting ties" with the relationship.

Survivor

Survival mode is a mode we all often live in. It's what we do to cope and get by when we feel like we are treading water. In the early stages of my current company, I was in survival mode. I was checking off boxes, having some success, and attending all that I could. While experiencing some success, I was more in learning and management mode than work mode. It took attending that first Breakthrough Mastermind to realize all that I wasn't doing... Leaving that weekend could have paralyzed me. I easily could have gone home and stayed in overwhelm. I could have decided it was a great weekend, with great learning, but the work wasn't for me... It was a bit overwhelming to realize there was so much I wasn't doing and so much I needed to do better. But instead, I dove into Conqueror's Mindset. I knew the work would be worth it.

Conqueror

I let all the fears subside. I waved goodbye to all the thoughts of "I'm not sure I can actually do this". I told myself, I would figure it out. I knew I had resources such as mentors, coaches, friends, and books to turn to.

I'd been a Conqueror before I even knew what a Conqueror was! I was able to attend my company's first Convention, and they announced the next company trip. I was determined to earn that trip. Convention was in September and in October of every year, and my husband has to submit his vacation time for the entire NEXT year. I told him the dates and told him to request them off! He has 3 rounds of this and he didn't request these dates off on his first round, telling me the family road trip was more important. True, I get it. 2nd round, he didn't take the dates off, using some other reason. This one was not so believable for me. 3rd round comes along and he admits he doesn't want to take the time off when it wasn't a guaranteed thing. Ding, ding, ding. If I wasn't SURE I was going to earn it before, I was then!

By March it was looking so possible. By end of April, I had the minimum amount of points but only in two of the three categories. I was *so* disappointed. But only for a couple of days because I then received a call being INVITED on the Company Trip!!!! I believed I could make it happen. I believed it was possible. And I put in the work to make it happen. Had I given up halfway thru, that invitation would not have been extended. My efforts were recognized and rewarded.

(My husband had to make some arrangements with coworkers, and it was a bit tricky, but he was able to get the time off! Since then, he has believed I will do everything I say I'll do and has been my biggest supporter!)

What is so very important is to understand is that we all will experience Victim and Survivor moments. The beauty is that you will overcome and not stay there for as long as you used to. The overcoming part gets better and easier. Conqueror mindset will eventually trump Victim and Survivor if you believe in yourself and put in the work.

"Your trauma is valid.

Even if other people have experienced "worse".

Even if someone else who went through the same experience doesn't feel debilitated by it.

Even if it "could have been avoided".

Even if it happened a long time ago.

Even if no one knows.

Your trauma is real and valid and you deserve a space to talk about it.

It isn't desperate or pathetic or attention-seeking.

It's self-care.

It's inconceivably brave.

And regardless of the magnitude of your struggle, you're allowed to take care of yourself by

processing and unloading some of the pain you carry.

Your pain matters. Your experience matters. And your healing matters. Nothing and no one can take that away."

~Daniell Koepke

7

Traumas

What does the word trauma mean to you? I used to believe it represented big, life-changing, sad events, like a death. But trauma has many different faces. It can be a betrayal, it can be a hurt. It can occur within any form of abuse; mental, emotional, physical, and sexual.

The more I grow up, the more I see that many people are *living* in their trauma. This is not a safe or peaceful place, but they are in survival mode.

Traumas need to be healed. That healing can come in many different forms but must happen in order to live an intentionally peace-filled life.

I experienced a trauma when I gave birth to our second child. Our first kiddo's birth was a beautiful and "easy" experience. So, I didn't go into the second with any concerns or hesitations.

Long story short, I ended up in an emergency c-section. As they wheeled me out of my hospital room, and into the emergency surgery room, my husband was not with me. I remember asking for him, to make sure he was coming. I'm confident I had gone into shock once the nurse told me something was wrong with my baby, and they needed to perform an emergency c-section.

I couldn't stop shaking.
I couldn't think straight.
Everything became slow motion.
Everything became blurry.

My recovery was nothing like after having my first. And every time I saw that scar below my belly button I felt anger. I'm not an angry person. I never felt anger towards my baby. I was extremely grateful that she got here safe. But I felt like my body had betrayed me. I know many people with health issues often feel this way. Feeling like your body is broken or has betrayed you can be a trauma in your life.

At my 6-week follow-up appointment, my doctor congratulated me and told me that was the fastest she'd seen anyone recover from a c-section. I was proud, but I was still so angry.

It took years to let go of that anger. It took years to heal. I chose gratitude over anger. One day I looked down and thought, "How did I get that scar?" It was pretty funny, actually!!! But that was how

I knew I'd healed. I'd moved on. I'd let go of the anger I'd carried for so long. I believe it was a matter of where my focus was. I stopped focusing on the scar. I stopped focusing on my anger. And after enough time, I'd legitimately forgotten why it was there.

Our traumas can be a detriment or a growth opportunity. I hope you choose growth and healing.

"Identify your problems, but give your power and energy to solutions."

~Tony Robbins

"Where focus goes, energy flows."

~Tony Robbins

"Your energy is contagious."

~Anonymous

"I remind myself that I am exactly where and who I am supposed to be right now. And so are others. I can only do what I can do right here and now. I can only choose for myself. My space and energy deserve and require my assistance. I choose to wish well on those that it is TIME to release. For both our benefits. For the greater good. I am open to receiving the outcome. I allow myself to grieve the loss of this person, place, thing and the former self that chose them. Nothing is permanent. I can change my mind at any time. I choose to honor my boundaries. By doing so I am an example to those and that which I am creating the boundary for. I honor my intuition. I choose to let go."

~Jamy Grogan

8

Energy

Have you ever noticed the energy in a room shift??? In the last few years, I've come to learn that I am an empath. For some of you that word may seem strange, hokey, or foreign. But I will tell you the more I've embraced it, the more I recognize and am grateful for the insights it gives me. I can sense when someone is lonely, uncomfortable, frustrated, or upset. When I was younger this was quite overwhelming because I would tend to take on the emotions of others without realizing it. Now, when I sense them, I don't have to take them on as my own. I can acknowledge where they are coming from and hold space for that.

If you are like me and can sense and recognize the emotions of others, it is SO very important to protect your peace. This might mean walking away, this might mean cutting ties, and this might mean having to prepare yourself when you know you have to interact with draining or negative persons. Building boundaries is necessary. Know yourself well enough to know when, how, and with who to protect yourself from.

I've found water to be therapeutic. Whether showering, bathing, being at a pool, the lake, waterfall, or ocean, or even just listening to the sound of water, brings me peace and contentment!!! Find ways to release and let go of the emotions and/or energies that need to be let go. Energy cleansing is a wonderful and beautiful modality resource.

I have a brother who struggles with mental health and addictions. It's been a difficult journey with him. There have been times he's been very much a part of my life, and times, when we have minimal interaction. While hard, difficult, and at times very sad, this has been a necessary and healthy boundary for me. He often spirals. For many, many years, I'd get caught up in the spiral with him. I've learned to protect my energy. I've learned that I can love and hold space for him and his experiences without getting tangled up in his emotions and struggles. Without feeling like there is some responsibility I have to make life easier for him.

I think it's very important to identify where the emotions we feel are coming from. Are they from within us, or others around us?

If from others, identifying who and holding space for them, and recognizing it's theirs to process is a part of building a boundary. As a recovering "fixer" this was a huge hurdle I found necessary to overcome. Because I could feel and sense it, I felt I could also help "fix" it. Holding space and placing responsibility where it belonged, helped lead me to so much peace.

If within us, figuring out why and where it came from, can help us process and move forward.

Recently our air conditioning stopped working. This was during summer, and terrible timing. I scheduled a tune-up with a company. This company came while I wasn't home, and told my husband our 5-year-old home required a total upgrade that would cost us almost $15,000. When I did get home and my husband and this young man shared with me the situation, I was immediately frustrated. Yes, it was a lot of money and I didn't want to pay that, also, my home was not old enough to need a whole new upgrade. But this kid had convinced my husband that because we'd finished our basement later, it wasn't able to do the job we needed it to do.

I told my husband no and the guy no, and told my husband we'd get a second opinion. The kid got on the phone with his boss and kept getting my husband a better deal. This happened twice. The second time, was an even better deal than the first. I'd told my husband to decide, but thought the cost would turn him away. But he was convinced this was necessary.

Thankfully, we have an old friend and neighbor in the air conditioning industry and I quickly reached out to him. He told me to not pay for anything. So, I told my husband to tell this kid no, pay him for the tune-up and send him on his way.

We ended up having his trusted friend come over to take a look. It ended up being a $120 fix.

It took me a bit, but I realized when I sense dishonesty or feel like we're being taken advantage of, my energy goes into high gear and I get upset. Even angry. In recognizing this, I was able to look back on other situations where I'd responded in ways that weren't typical for me. It made sense.

Your energy can sense intention.

Listen to your energy. Trust your intuition. Let it guide you and warn you. It may not make sense, right away, or ever. The more you listen, the more awareness you'll receive.

"You will continue to suffer if you have an emotional reaction to everything that is said to you. True power is sitting back and observing things with magic. True power is restraint. If words control you that means everyone else can control you. Breathe and allow things to pass."

~Warren Buffet

9

❧

Reaction

I have a 24-hour rule. It has helped me a *lot* of times and in many different situations.

If something stirs a strong emotional response within you, wait 24 hours before confronting or responding.

This is not easy. Especially if you are passionate, a defender, or a protector. But that 24 hours may give you perspective and insight that you don't always have when triggered.

The first time I heard about this 24-hour rule was from my oldest child's soccer coach. He encouraged us as parents to apply the 24 hour rule after soccer games. He expressed that he didn't want phone calls right after games about how much playing time our child did or didn't get. If in 24 hours we were still upset, reach out and he'd be happy to have a conversation with us.

This rule has helped me in relationships, friendships, business, and as a sports parent!

Are you quick to anger?
Do you recognize that you have quick emotional reactions to situations?

We all have triggers. They often come from emotional childhood experiences where we felt out of control in the situation we were in.

Recognizing our reactions and becoming intentional in our behavior is important. Often people just react as if they are not in control. But we *are* in control of our actions, behaviors, and reactions. Take ownership and responsibility. Take pride in who you are and how you behave. This will bring you so much peace. It will be hard at first but so worth it.

I recently had an experience where I completely lost it. I'm a Christian woman who will use a "hell" and a "damn" every now and then to be funny or make a point, but I'm not one to fly off the handle and cuss!

I was watching my second oldest's soccer game and there was a moment between her and the goalie... My daughter ended up flipping over the top of the goalie and landing on her neck/back.

For me, this all happened in slow motion. It was so scary. This is my kiddo that gets knocked down and always pops up super quick. But she wasn't popping up. The ref walked *past* her, barely checking on her and I am pretty sure I had an out-of-body experience... I dropped the F-bomb 3 or 4 times...

I've done YEARS of personal development. I teach and train about reactions, emotions, and behavior, and here I go losing my biscuits in front of both teams of 14-year-old girls, parents, siblings, and coaches.

After getting red-carded and told to leave the field, I could not stop shaking. As I walked away and realized what I'd just done, I was *beyond* embarrassed. After the game, the refs had left, and I knew I needed to go back and apologize to my own kid and husband, whom I was SURE I'd totally embarrassed. I also knew I needed to apologize to the girls on her team, the parents, and the coaches, whom I consider friends.

It was a moment I'd wished I could totally erase. I was so disappointed in myself. I couldn't believe I lost control like that. However... It happened. And I knew I needed to own up to it. While I wasn't proud of it, I had to recognize that it didn't take away or undo all the good things I've learned over the past 5 years. At first, I did believe all the good I'd learned had just been flushed away. Gone.

We are human, and I had a human/momma bear moment. I was scared for my daughter's safety and angry that she didn't get checked on.

I've had to remind myself here and there that while I did lose it, I also did own up to it and made the necessary and needed apologies.

In life, we are going to make mistakes. We are going to handle things poorly.

I have people in my life who refuse to apologize. So, apologizing is very important to me. I apologize to my kids when I know I've hurt their feelings. I apologize to my husband. I'm so grateful they are forgiving.

Some people feel like an apology is losing power. It's not. It's building respect.

Recognizing and taking ownership gets us so much further than blaming or making excuses. To have a peace-filled life we need to forgive ourselves and show ourselves grace in the times we fall short.

"Be the person you want to have in your life."

~Anonymous

"Never walk away from connections that touch the deepest parts of your soul."

~Prince Madness

IO

Connection

I crave connection. While I know not all people are that way, I believe our souls need connection. Whether with a few people or with many, is very individual.

The experiences we have in relating with and connecting with others can add so much warmth, positivity, and value to our lives.

We need the opportunity to relate with others or be validated in our circumstances.

I often question how I came from my parents! My parents are completely content to keep to themselves. Then there's me. I grew up away from extended family and back in the days when talking on the phone long-distance cost money... so relationships and connections with grandparents, cousins, aunts, and uncles weren't active in my life...

I've been blessed to find adopted families in the different places we have lived! We now live near family and still, I seek out connections! We built our dream home and I remember feeling like my adventures of moving and making new connections were over...but then I got into this really incredible industry of network marketing! Through my company and attending Masterminds, I've been able to continue making connections with new people! What I thought was over, was the beginning and has actually expanded in unexpected ways!!! And I love it!

I recently spent time at a camp for girls ages 12-17. It was one of 15 I've attended as both an adult and a youth. It was probably the best I've ever experienced. Both leaders and girls all got along. It was uplifting, positive, and wonderful. My heart, my spirit, my soul needed this. I was able to be with my 3 daughters and my Dad. I was able to disconnect from the outside world. I was able to process some thoughts and feelings. I was able to connect with nature, which always helps me feel closer to God. I was able to ask myself some very important questions. I'd been doubting myself based on failed relationships with people I'd hoped would be life-long, positive, uplifting connections. The connections I experienced with the youth and fellow leaders were blessings in my life and came at a much-needed time.

I was recently telling someone how much I adored and admired them, and her response was, "I'm not for everyone." That has stuck with me for months. As a recovering people pleaser, that's been a hard one to swallow as an adult. I know and acknowledge that I don't personally like or love everyone I meet. So, why would I expect or hope for everyone to like or love me?

I'm not for everyone.

While I'm not for everyone, there are those that do and will embrace me, accept me, welcome me, and call me a friend. Those are the people I want to be around. Those are the people I choose to surround myself with.

We get to choose who we spend time with. Where we put our energy. If a connection is something you crave, be sure to also be the person you want to be around.

The majority of my business is run on social media! I have a passion for people, so my desire to connect has always been something I enjoy, look forward to, and do not feel is a chore.

Last week, I met my future best friend on social media. I don't know how long we've been "friends", I don't know who friended who, but we introduced ourselves and I'll tell you, we have so much in common. We ended up talking back and forth for 2 hours!!! People may judge this and I will tell you, let them. You do you. The truth is people will judge no matter what, but also they think about you less often than you may think.

Connections can be such a gift! It may not always look the way you think it would or "should". Embrace it in whatever form it comes in!

"Self Confidence is a super power. Once you start to believe in yourself, magic starts happening."

~Unknown

"Attention with the Right Intention."

~Rob Sperry

I I

Aligning Public, Private, and Secret Self

Most days before my kids leave for school I say to them, "Remember who you are." On occasion, I've felt compelled to ask them, "Do you know who you are?"

So, I ask **you**, "Do you know who **you** are?"

As we discuss how to align our public, private, and secret self, awareness is going to play a big role!!!! You can choose to dig deep, and be brutally honest with yourself, or... you can stay right where you are at and consider this a "decent read" with "good information that doesn't apply" to you!

Public

When I was a young Mom, I was a youth leader for young women ages 12-18!!! There were girls in my neighborhood that would come hang out with me and my kids and I LOVED these moments!!!! I wanted them to feel safe, welcome, and cared about!!! I would laugh and tease and keep things light!

It was several months of this when one day all the friends had left and I went and hid in my room away from my own kids.

As I was sitting in my room, my oldest came in and asked if I would play a game with her. I made some excuse and I remember her leaving my room looking so disappointed. I had the thought, "why am I more willing to play games, watch movies, and hang out when other kids are here, but not when it's with just my kids?" I would talk nicer to my own kids and was more careful about my reactions when other kids were around. Why? I immediately felt immense guilt. I started remembering the times I'd pepped up or gotten happy because friends had come over...All the times I'd drop whatever I was doing to pay attention to the neighborhood kids.

I decided right then, that was not the Mom I hoped to be or wanted to be. I wanted to be the loving, fun Mom always, not just when friends were around.

So, take a moment and think, what ways do you behave, act, and react in public that would be different in front of your own family?

Private

I always had thought Private and Secret were the same. I was wrong. Your Private self is the person you allow your family members to see. Both those you live with, and extended family. This is where you may react more in front of them than you would in front of neighbors, coworkers, or friends.

What are the behaviors you feel safe showing in front of loved ones, but maybe not others?

My husband and I had gone on a trip, just the two of us, and in the last couple of days, he'd started to become grumpy. We got picked up at the airport by his coworker and during the drive, he was sharing how great the trip had been. We got to his work and he was positive, laughing, joking, and happy. I have a husband that I loooove, but I got upset when I saw how he was around his coworkers. He was a totally different person than who we get at home. He was giving his best self to them. Why??? Don't we, as his wife and kids, deserve the best side of him? While the answer is yes, it's easier said than done.

The reason this is often the case in our families, in our homes, is a safe place. We know there are ways we can behave and act and still be loved. So, we keep a tighter hold on our behavior at places like work or around friends and neighbors.

While a lot of this is human nature, it's still something to become aware of and try to give the best of ourselves to our families.

Secret

Secret self. This is often the hardest to bring to the surface. Who are you when you are alone? Your mind is powerful. What are you telling yourself? What are the voices in your head saying? Are you kind? Critical? Are you hard on yourself? Do you extend yourself grace?

My guess is at different times you are all of these things.

Does it depend on your mood? How you slept? The dreams you had? The plan for the day/week? If you have something to look forward to?

Your secret self is the aspect of your life you keep to yourself. Your deepest insecurities. The most difficult battles that rage within you. The places your mind goes when you are down, struggling, and feeling like you are treading water.

You may be starting to ask, how in the world do these align???

There are going to be things I share with my husband that I wouldn't share with a stranger on social media! However, we must remember to not allow shame to keep us from being who we are.

Remember who **you** are.

Each day we are alive, we are in the process of becoming.

But becoming what?? Are you becoming your best self each day?

Only you can answer that.

Aligning is not easy. It might mean adding personal development. Maybe try having a theme week or month where you intentionally focus on qualities you want to improve. It might mean learning how to take responsibility for mistakes you make. Admitting when you are wrong. Apologizing. It's more about being better than being right.

Take the time to do some self-assessment. Ask close family members if they feel you change around different groups of people. Their answers might surprise you and might initially hurt your feelings, but take it in stride and let go of your ego and recognize the changes you want to make.

Too often we make changes for others, but those don't usually stick. We have to want to make the change for ourselves. To improve our peace and lead a more fulfilling life.

When people meet me on social media, then meet me in person, the biggest compliment is for them to tell me I'm who they expected me to be! I have a presence on social media for work! I don't ever want to come across as perfect, or like I have it all together, or all the answers, because I don't!!!!!! But I take pride in being me regardless of where I am or who I am with.

Aligning your public, private, and secret self will bring you so much peace. Your confidence will improve because there will be less you feel like you have to hide! Your energy will boost because you'll no longer be putting on a show! Your relationships will blossom because you will be a safe place for others. They will sense the strength and truth and light within you.

"What if you're everything that you think that you're not. And nothing that you think that you are?"

~Steph Purpura

12

Living Your Truth

What is truth? A common saying lately is to "speak your truth" or "live your truth"!! We live in a social media world, where we are easily able to express our ideas, thoughts, and opinions!!! What's one person's truth, doesn't make it another person's truth.

We ◇◇◇◇, honor, respect, and hold space for that. We have come to believe our truth is everyone's. It's not.

Truth in this sense is not staying true to its definition. By definition, truth is: facts that can be proven. But, the fact is we as humans are constantly changing. So, living our most true, authentic self will change as we are learning, growing, experiencing, and evolving.

We also need to take into account, perception, and perspective. Let's say ten people witness an accident and are asked to give their accounts. You most likely will have ten different versions of what happened. Each person may be coming from different viewpoints. Or it may have happened so quickly that each person's brain focused on a different aspect. The point is, that what is true to you and what you believe to have happened may be similar and yet appear different to others.

As I write this, I have to ask myself. Am I living my truth? In what ways?

I am part of a faith/religion where there is a big focus on family. The hard part is not all family relationships are healthy. A year ago, I severed an extended family tie. While I admit, that I may not have done it in a mature way, I don't regret it. I didn't want any questions about the future of the relationship. As I've had years of personal growth and worked a lot in personal development, I started to recognize this particular relationship was not healthy and was holding me back. For years I was in a lose/lose situation. I couldn't do anything right and enough was never enough. I had this insane belief that if I just did this, or that, it would earn me points with this person. Eventually, my husband and I came to find that we were pieces on a game board. We didn't know the goals, expectations, or rules. We decided to take our pieces off the gameboard and quit playing the game.

Maybe you have a person in your life with whom you can relate. This person would ask me a question and before I could even answer was telling me their answer to the same question. I began to realize that to "Live my truth", this person could not remain in my life. I was wasting time and energy in a relationship that wasn't serving me. Years ago, shame and guilt would have followed me as though I hadn't done enough... The truth was, it was never going to be enough. If you can relate to any of this, I encourage you to read, "But It's Your Family" by Dr. Sherrie Campbell.

I feel the best way I can live my truth is to be authentically me. I chose to give myself grace when and where needed. I came to this earth with my unique spirit, energy, and personality. Keep in mind, personality isn't permanent. Much of what makes me, me, and who I am...I'm proud of.

Living your truth might be hard. Might be uncomfortable. Might mean disconnecting. But in order to live your life to the fullest and to live in peace, this is a must.

"Remember, despite how open, peaceful and loving you attempt to be, people can only meet you as deeply as they've met themselves."

~Matt Kahn

13

Bless and Release

There will come times in your life when setting healthy boundaries isn't enough. Letting people go might become necessary. The cutting of ties is sometimes followed by guilt. It's important that we make this decision not out of spite or malice, but out of the protection of our peace.

In business, there are times that people will choose to leave. As humans, we tend to take this personally or as a rejection. It's easier said than done, but it's so much better to bless and release. You never know what the future holds and what role that person may play in your future.

I remember when my first teammate chose to go another

direction. I felt like I'd failed this person. But in reality, people's lives change. People come and go. That's their right and their choice. Wishing them well and understanding that we each have our own path and journey and respecting that is key.

As I mentioned before, I have a brother that tends to come and go from my life. My hope is that in the "coming" he always knows he is welcome and loved.

Ultimately, we have to remember it's not usually about us. Choices get made for reasons beyond what we often know or are told. All we can do is do our best. If we bless and release with positive feelings of wishing others well, it will keep the other negative feelings out of our hearts. Negativity doesn't serve us and doesn't bring us peace.

"True peace is knowing God is in control."

~Anonymous

14

Peace in Christ

There's a song I love called "Peace in Christ". I encourage all of you that have a belief and faith in Christ to look it up. Ultimately, He is where we can find peace. All the topics I've touched on can be helpful and valuable tools. And I hope they've given you direction. We often look for outward sources, but He is the ultimate giver of Peace.

He gives us hope
When hope is gone
He gives us strength
When we can't go on
He gives us shelter
In the storms of life

When there's no peace on Earth
There is peace in Christ.

Thank you for taking the time to read this and I hope you will connect with me on Social Media!